MIGRATION AND REFUGEES

Cath Senker

Contents

Introduction

Throughout history, people migrated to other countries. They fled to escape war and natural disasters, or traveled with a pioneering spirit to seek better farmland or prospects. We now live in an era of globalization, in which countries are becoming more closely linked together through the growth of trade, communications, travel, and culture. It has made moving between places much easier. International travel has become cheaper, and improved communications make people increasingly aware of lifestyles in foreign countries. More people are moving from less economically developed countries (LEDCs) to more economically developed countries (MEDCs). Is the resulting mixing of cultures a good thing, expanding knowledge and tolerance? Or does globalization in migration damage the economies and societies of the countries involved?

Legal Migrants

There are many kinds of migration. Some people can move legally to another country. For instance, Suekran Ezgimen left Turkey

▲ These Poles at a Polish job fair in London are finding out about employment as taxi drivers. Many Polish migrants to the United Kingdom have good English language skills and can take on a variety of jobs.

as a young woman to work in the Siemens engineering factory in Berlin, Germany. Now working as a dance teacher, she has settled permanently. She is an immigrant to Germany (and an emigrant from Turkey).

Przemek Ocinski came to Edinburgh, Scotland from Poland and found a job as a chef. He is one of about 350,000 Poles who came to work in the United Kingdom (the UK) between 2004 and 2006. The majority stay for a while and then return home. They are migrants. Other kinds of migrants include contract workers, who take a job in another country for a certain time. Some migrants are professionals who work for transnational companies (businesses that operate in several different nations), and move from country to country. People who move within their own country are also called migrants.

Undocumented Migrants

Some people are not able to migrate legally. Mexicans are not allowed to move freely to the neighboring United States. Christina, from southern Mexico, paid a smuggler more than $6,000 to sneak her across the border, avoiding armed patrols and enduring a long, hot trek across the desert. She is an undocumented migrant, or illegal immigrant. Not all undocumented migrants enter a country illegally. Some come as students or temporary workers but stay after their visa has run out, and become illegal immigrants.

Refugees

Refugees flee their country to escape persecution (unfair treatment) because of their religion, race, or membership of a particular social group. They usually flee with no passport or official documents. On arrival they seek a refuge—safety from danger.

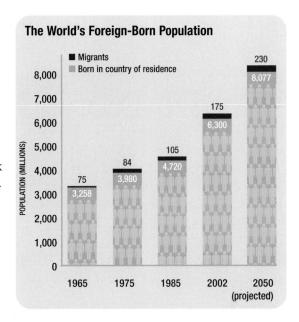

The World's Foreign-Born Population

- ■ Migrants
- ■ Born in country of residence

▲ This bar chart shows that the great majority of people live in their country of birth, but that the proportion of migrants is growing.

Focus on...
Where Do Migrants Go?

According to the United Nations, in 2005 about 191 million people—around three percent of the world's population—lived outside their country of birth. Of the 36 million who migrated between 1990 and 2005, 33 million reached MEDCs. Yet 90 percent of refugees (who make up seven percent of all migrants) live in LEDCs.

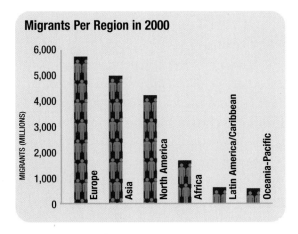

Migrants Per Region in 2000

▲ This chart shows the number of migrants in different regions of the world.

Why Do People Migrate?

Writers on migration often talk about the "push and pull factors" that encourage people to migrate. Push factors are bad things in people's home countries that persuade them to leave. Pull factors are the advantages offered by moving to another country.

Push Factors

People may be living through war or suffering from poverty or persecution in their home countries. For instance, there are around 26 million Kurds, mostly living in Turkey, Iran, Iraq, and parts of Syria and Armenia. With their own languages and culture, they would like their own independent Kurdish state. The governments of those countries have resisted their demands. This has led to conflict in the region, which has forced many thousands of Kurds to flee as refugees. Only a minority of people who experience such push factors manage to flee, though. However terrible their situation, it is an incredibly difficult and expensive decision to leave everything behind.

Pull Factors

Pull factors are the positive things that encourage people to migrate to a new country, such as more freedom, a better standard of living, and good schools for their children. It is not only people in LEDCs that move; some northern Europeans migrate to Spain to enjoy the pleasant weather and relaxed lifestyle. The biggest pull factor is the prospect of a job— most migrants move for work. Migrants are usually young, fit people and not the poorest, who cannot afford to move anywhere.

▲ These Mexican migrants are working as flower pickers in California. The U.S. is a popular destination for migrants, particularly those from Mexico.

▲ A family of Kosovar-Albanians return to Kosovo in the summer of 1999, just after the end of the three-month war between the Serbs and the Kosovo Liberation Army. Despite the dangers from unexploded land mines (bombs lying on the ground), they are glad to be home.

Return Migration

Migration is often temporary. Many migrants want to return home when the conflict in their home country is over or they have made money in another country for a few years. After the end of the Kosovo War in 1998, many refugees rapidly returned—even though they knew their homes had been destroyed. According to research, only about 30 percent of Mexican migrants in the United States remain in the country for more than 10 years. Much attention is given to the arrival of migrants, but little is given to the fact that many return.

Eyewitness

"I come from Konin in central Poland. I took six weeks' paid holiday [vacation] from my job as a nurse and drove 600 km (373 miles) to work on a farm in Beelitz, Germany. During my time there, I'll earn £2,000 ($2,700), the same as I earn in six months at the hospital. I like to work and I'd like a better life in Poland, so that I'm not just living month to month."

Ms. Pawlak, *Christian Science Monitor*, May 14, 2006

▲ Four generations of a family who were all slaves in South Carolina. Slavery was abolished in the United States in 1865. The ancestors of most African-Americans living there today were slaves.

A Brief History of Migration

The push and pull factors that drive migration have always existed. Before the 16th century, groups of people often moved to conquer territory. They generally settled and mixed with the local inhabitants. From around the year 1500, improvements in technology made it easier for people to sail long distances. For the following 300 years, large numbers of people left Europe and took control of the American continent and the Caribbean. They killed a large proportion of the native populations and most of the rest died from disease. However, the Europeans needed workers to farm the large plantations they founded there. From 1500 to 1870, Europeans seized a vast number of Africans as slaves—perhaps 12 million. They forced the Africans to migrate to the Americas to work for them under cruel conditions.

Europeans themselves continued to migrate from 1850 to 1950, mostly to North America, Australia, and New Zealand. The majority moved for a better life. Then, in the late 19th and early 20th centuries, some countries started to bring in immigration controls to restrict the number of immigrants.

This was especially the case during the Great Depression, the economic crisis of the 1930s. The situation changed once more after the end of World War II in 1945, when Europe needed foreign workers to rebuild economies shattered during the war. There was mass migration from Asia, Africa, and the Caribbean to Europe. From the 1960s onward, North America and Australia also needed labor, and opened their doors to migrants from all over the world.

Refugee Crises

Throughout history, people have been forced to leave their countries as refugees. For example, the Jewish people have repeatedly

▼ These survivors at the end of World War II in 1945 cook a meal amid the ruins of the town of Nuremberg, Germany.

migrated to avoid persecution. During World War II, about 60 million Europeans in Nazi-occupied Europe lost their homes, the largest number of refugees yet seen. Since then, there have been many other wars, creating waves of refugees. The 1960s and 1970s saw struggles in European colonies for independence from their rulers, followed by crises in Asia during the 1970s, such as the Vietnam War. Since then, serious conflicts in Afghanistan, Rwanda, Somalia, and many other places have caused millions to flee.

Focus on...
The Convention on the Status of Refugees

After World War II, an international system was created to protect refugees. The 1951 Convention on the Status of Refugees defined a refugee as a person who has fled from his or her country and is unable to return "owing to a well-founded fear of being persecuted for reasons of race, religion, nationality, membership in a particular social group or political opinion." It listed refugees' rights and the duty of countries to offer them refuge.

Escaping Danger: Refugees and Internally Displaced Persons

In 2005, there were 12.7 million people classified as refugees in the world. Refugees are forced to migrate because of danger in their own country. The majority travel to the nearest safer land, trekking long distances carrying small children and a few possessions. Most come from LEDCs and go to other LEDCs; the continents of Africa and Asia receive four-fifths of the world's refugees. Even larger numbers—about 25 million in 2006—flee within their own country and are known as Internally Displaced Persons (IDPs). Different countries have varying policies regarding the acceptance of refugees.

Origin	Main Countries of Asylum	Total (2006)
Afghanistan	Pakistan, Iran, Germany, Netherlands, UK	1,908,100
Sudan	Chad, Uganda, Kenya, Ethiopia, Central African Republic	693,300
Burundi	Tanzania, Democratic Republic of Congo, Rwanda, South Africa, Zambia	438,700
Dem. Rep. Congo	Tanzania, Zambia, Congo, Rwanda, Uganda	430,600
Somalia	Kenya, Yemen, UK, the U.S., Ethiopia	394,800
Vietnam	China, Germany, the U.S., France, Switzerland	358,200
Palestinians	Saudi Arabia, Egypt, Iraq, Libya, Algeria	349,700
Iraq	Iran, Germany, Netherlands, Syria, UK	262,100
Azerbaijan	Armenia, Germany, the U.S., Netherlands, France	233,700
Liberia	Sierra Leone, Guinea, Ivory Coast, Ghana, the U.S.	231,100

▲ This chart shows the origins of the largest refugee populations. Most of the countries have suffered from long-lasting conflict.

War

Most of the countries of origin, such as Afghanistan, have suffered continuous war for decades. The USSR invaded and occupied Afghanistan in 1979, causing six million Afghans to flee to neighboring Iran and Pakistan, where they stayed in vast refugee camps. Local forces fought the Soviet army for a decade until they drove it out in 1989. There was now no strong government, and various forces struggled to control the country. By 1996, an extreme Islamic group, the Taliban, had seized power. Then in 2001, anti-government groups and a U.S.-led international force crushed the Taliban government, creating further waves of refugees. At this time, Iran and Pakistan tried to stop further Afghans from entering their countries.

▲ Between 1979 and 1992, more than one-fifth of Afghanistan's population was forced to flee as refugees.

In 2007, Afghanistan was still in chaos. The new government formed after the fall of the Taliban could not control the country. The Taliban had regrouped and was resisting the government. There remained 1.9 million Afghan refugees outside Afghanistan and 140,000 displaced people within the country.

Have Your Say

Some people believe that the issue of refugees concerns everybody, while others feel that it is not their problem.

- If there are wars in other countries, should the people there sort out their own problems?
- Should governments be taking responsibility for helping refugees, rather than ordinary people?
- If we became refugees, would we expect people to help us? Should we then care for others who are less fortunate than we are?

Eyewitness

"Some claim that they have been personally attacked by armed militia, while others say they fled because their neighbors were killed and they feared a similar fate. People crossing the border generally suffer from extreme fatigue and many children appear malnourished."

UNHCR spokesperson Ron Redmond, describing the arrival of Somali refugees in Dadaab refugee camp, Kenya, in September 2006

Suffering in Somalia

Somalia in eastern Africa has also been ripped apart by war. Since 1991, it has been without a strong government. There have been years of fighting between rival clans, as well as terrible famine and disease. Armed fighters attack, rape, and maim civilians who are members of a different clan. Approximately one million died between 1991 and 2006. A new government was set up in 2004, but had little power. By mid-2006, an Islamic force had taken control of much of the south, but government troops, with Ethiopia's help, defeated it by the end of the year. During 2006, over 26,000 Somali refugees, mostly women and children, walked to Kenya to avoid the fighting between the Islamic forces and the various clans.

▲ These Somali refugees fled the civil war in Somalia and are living in makeshift huts in the Dadaab refugee camp.

Internally Displaced Persons

Like refugees, IDPs have left their homes because of conflict or persecution. But unlike refugees, they have not crossed into another country. Even though they face similar difficulties to refugees—and there are twice as many of them—their plight receives less attention. The vast majority of displaced people move within LEDCs.

Country	Number of IDPs (2006)
Colombia	1.9–3.8 million
Iraq	1.7 million
Democratic Republic of the Congo	1.1 million
Algeria	1 million (EU estimate, 2002)
India	at least 600,000
Azerbaijan	578,545–686,586
Bangladesh	500,000
Lebanon	216,000–800,000

▲ This chart shows the countries with the highest estimated numbers of IDPs.

Focus on...
Child IDPs and Refugees

- Children make up about half of the world's refugees and IDPs; the majority are victims of war.
- Many child refugees are orphans or have been separated from their parents.
- Child refugees usually go hungry and receive no education.
- Over 300,000 children under 18—many under 10—are seized by armies to serve as soldiers. Most are in Africa.

Civil War in Sudan

In the 1970s, an Islamic government imposed Islamic law in Sudan, which was opposed by the mainly Christian south. The Sudanese People's Liberation Army (SPLA) formed to fight for an independent southern Sudan. Civil war broke out in 1983, and millions

were displaced within Sudan or left as refugees. Finally, in 2005, a peace agreement was signed by the government and the SPLA.

Other rebel groups did not agree to peace, though. Civil war continued, especially in Darfur in western Sudan, where armed groups continued to fight the government. In Darfur, both government and rebel forces attacked civilians. They killed men, raped women, burned down their homes, and stole their crops and cattle. In 2006, there remained over 5 million displaced people in Sudan, including 1.8 million in Darfur alone.

▼ These Sudanese refugees are crossing a river to escape the violence in Darfur. They are heading for one of the refugee camps in neighboring Chad.

Eyewitness

A young woman described the start of her ordeal when her village in Kabkabiya district, Darfur, was attacked by the Janjawid, a fighting group supported by the government:

"In May 2003, they dropped bombs from Antonovs [Russian-made aircraft used by the Sudanese government] on our cattle and on our huts. We were hiding near the village and were going back to the village at night to sleep there until June/July. Then they attacked the village. It was in the morning, I was preparing breakfast when I saw them coming. They started shooting. They came with horses and cars and they were all in uniforms. They killed my husband Musa Harun Arba. I ran and left the village. I took my three children and two children of my neighbor and we ran to Hara, the village in the valley."
Amnesty International, 2004

▲ This is a Roma settlement in Slovakia. The Roma are among the poorest people in all of eastern Europe. They suffer racism at the hands of officials, such as the police, as well as from ordinary people.

Persecution

Even if there is no war going on, members of ethnic minority groups may be persecuted by the government and the majority population. If life becomes unbearable, they may be forced to leave as refugees.

The Roma are an ethnic minority group mainly living in eastern European countries, such as Poland, Romania, and the Slovak Republic. In the past, they were traveling people who lived in caravans and spoke their own language. In most countries nowadays, they suffer from racism, poor living conditions, unemployment, and even violence.

Opposing the Government

Some people have to leave their country because they have spoken out against a government that does not allow opposition. If they do not leave, their lives are in danger. In Zimbabwe, the government of Robert Mugabe has tried to stop any opposition to its policies. Since 2002, leaders of the main opposition party, the Movement for Democratic Change (MDC), have been arrested and often violently attacked. Even local leaders and activists in the movement are arrested for holding meetings or peaceful protests against the government. The police disrupt their gatherings and beat them up or even shoot them. Because of this persecution, many MDC activists have had to escape from Zimbabwe.

Restricting Refugees

LEDCs have traditionally welcomed refugees who have fled war and persecution. Now, they often restrict them because it is hard to cope with the large numbers. Iran has a high proportion of refugees: 994,000 out of a population of 69.5 million (2006). The vast majority are from war-torn Afghanistan. In 2005, Iran deported, or sent home, 200,000 Afghans who did not have residence permits.

Eyewitness

Gerard and his family were members of the Movement for Democratic Change in Bulawayo, Zimbabwe. In 2000, Gerard was arrested after a protest rally against the government-backed invasion and occupation of farmers' land.

"I was taken to the police station . . . They started hitting me, beating me up and torturing me. They made me stand with my feet in a bucket of ice. They wanted names of the people I knew who were also members of the MDC. But they couldn't get anything out of me . . . [Later] some government supporters . . . stoned our family home . . . In the end it became too much for me and I decided to leave for the UK." **Refugee Council**

▲ In Zimbabwe, white farmers own the best land. In 2000, many farms owned by white people were invaded by government supporters. This led to conflict between white farmers and Mugabe's supporters, and a dramatic fall in agricultural production. It was an unsuccessful way to try to make land ownership more equal.

▼ An Iranian woman passes Afghan workers in Tehran removing election posters in 2005. The Iranian government no longer welcomes Afghan refugees, but in fact they are useful to the economy, usually doing manual work for low pay.

Seeking Asylum

Although only a minority of refugees come to MEDCs, these countries have brought in strict rules for claiming political asylum. Asylum seekers have to prove that they were persecuted and would face terrible danger if they returned to their own country. There are concerns that without such systems, there would be unmanageable numbers of refugees, which would place a huge burden on the receiving country. Australia has a particularly tough policy. All refugees are placed in detention centers while they make their claim to asylum. In other countries, such as the UK, most asylum seekers are not detained but may not work until their claim has been assessed.

Proof of Persecution

Asylum officials expect asylum seekers to prove they were persecuted, but this can be difficult to do. Refugees leave in a hurry without important documents, genuine passports, or visas. It is difficult to provide evidence of their situation from a distant country. Sometimes they do not speak the language of the host country, and may not

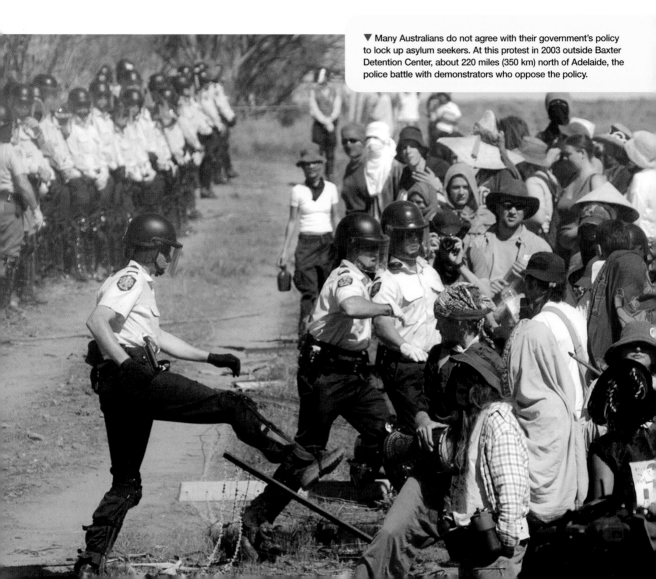

▼ Many Australians do not agree with their government's policy to lock up asylum seekers. At this protest in 2003 outside Baxter Detention Center, about 220 miles (350 km) north of Adelaide, the police battle with demonstrators who oppose the policy.

▲ This child came to the UK with his family after living for more than 10 years in a refugee camp. As part of a government program to resettle refugees, he has special English lessons.

have good translators. If they fail, they may be deported. Suleiman Dialo came to the UK from Guinea, West Africa. He left hastily after his parents, brothers and sisters had been murdered, and like many asylum seekers from West Africa, he had been tortured. Dialo spoke his own language, Fula, but no English and only broken French. With no local Fula speaker to interpret for him, he was unable to make his story convincing to asylum officials. He grew so desperate that rather than face deportation to Guinea, he killed himself by leaping from a Newcastle bridge.

Focus on...
Separated Children

Separated children are those under age 18 living outside their country of origin without a parent or guardian. They make up about half of all asylum seekers in MEDCs. With the same needs as other children, they may also be suffering from trauma. Perhaps they have witnessed horrific violence against family members or been attacked or abused themselves. In the U.S., separated children either go to live with relatives, if they have any, or a foster family. Otherwise, they are placed in a children's home.

Have Your Say

Some people argue that the number of asylum seekers entering a country should be restricted, while others believe it is our moral responsibility to protect all refugees.

- If all refugees are allowed in, will there be a shortage of housing, schools, and health care for the whole country?
- If one country is more generous than others, will vast numbers flock to that country?
- Should caring for people in fear of their lives be a high priority for governments?

Moving for a Better Life

The majority of migrants move for work. This is called labor migration. Many migrate within their own country, especially from rural areas to the cities. A great movement from rural to urban areas has been a feature of globalization. Yet if people cannot find a better job within their own country, they may try to find one in another. Labor migration abroad has also increased in the era of globalization. Most migrants move from LEDCs to MEDCs for better opportunities. Controls on immigration make it difficult to move legally to MEDCs, however, so many migrate illegally.

▲ This farmer in Nicaragua joined a fair-trade coffee cooperative and switched to growing organic coffee. He hopes that by growing high-quality coffee beans for a fair price he will earn a better living and be able to stay on his land.

Migration within Countries

One of the effects of globalization since 1990 has been a general decline in the world price of many agricultural products, such as cocoa, sugar, tea, and coffee. The economies of most LEDCs depend on selling these goods. The decrease in prices has had serious consequences for farmers in those countries. For example, large numbers of coffee farmers in traditional coffee-growing countries in Latin America have to sell their coffee beans for less money than they cost to grow. No longer able to make a decent living from the land, many sell out and move to the city, hoping to find a job.

Throughout the developing world, vast cities have mushroomed, with migrants living in homemade shacks in shanty towns, usually without running water or electricity. Yet for those pushed off the land, there may be no better option in their country.

▲ This is an aerial view of Paraisópolis, a shanty town in São Paolo, Brazil. In the background lies the wealthy area of Morumbi. São Paolo is one of the largest cities in the world and attracts huge numbers of migrants.

Migration between LEDCs

Some people migrate from one LEDC to another that is benefiting from globalization and has plenty of jobs. Many southern African migrants go to South Africa to work in the mines, on farms, and as craft and domestic workers. Chinese construction workers find jobs in South Korea. Saudi Arabia's wealth is based on oil production, but it does not have enough workers; one-fifth of the workforce are migrants.

Focus on...
Exploitation in Saudi Arabia

The largest migrant groups in Saudi Arabia are from the Indian subcontinent, the Philippines, and Indonesia. They may stay in the country to do a particular job and then have to return home. Some employers treat their migrant workers well, but others exploit them. Migrant workers from Bangladesh reported to a human rights organization that they had to work 10–12 hours a day, and sometimes through the night, repairing underground water pipes. They were not paid for the first two months. They did not dare complain for fear of losing their jobs and being deported.

Moving from LEDCs to MEDCs

Since the 1980s, in general MEDCs have become wealthier, and LEDCs relatively poorer. Some experts believe this is due to the effects of globalization, while others argue that it is because the benefits of globalization have not spread to all countries yet. The wealth gap means that migrants are drawn from LEDCs to MEDCs with growing economies and plenty of jobs.

Migrants tend to tread well-worn paths, going where there are already communities from their country. Many move from former colonies to the country that used to rule them because they share economic links and a common language. For instance, large Moroccan, Algerian, and Tunisian communities are found in France. Being geographically close is also an important factor in the choice of destination. The largest group of migrants in the U.S. is from Mexico, while Southeast Asian migrants generally make their way to Australia.

Changing Demographics

The United States and Australia are both countries that have been built on immigration. Since the 1960s, the United States has welcomed immigrants from all over the world. There are up to one million new immigrants a year; the U.S. population reached 288 million in 2005. The biggest proportion—14.5 percent in 2005—come from Latin America. There are 2.4 million Chinese Americans, forming the biggest group from Asia, while the Indian community has doubled over the past decade. The number of Vietnamese immigrants is also growing rapidly. According to population studies, by 2050, racial and ethnic minorities will

▲ Many large cities worldwide have a Chinatown, where Chinese residents have established restaurants, shops, and other businesses. There are several Chinatowns in the U.S., including this one in San Francisco.

outnumber non-Hispanic white people in the U.S.

Globalization has also lowered the cost of long distance flights and brought improved communications. It has become easier to organize a longer journey across continents, and more do so. In 2006, there were about 1.2 million legal immigrants from Latin America in Spain, plus many thousands of undocumented migrants.

The Expanding European Union

Political changes also affect migration. In 2004, the European Union (EU) expanded from 15 to 25 countries to include many eastern European nations, as well as Malta and Cyprus. Romania and Bulgaria joined the union in 2007. There has been an explosion of migration from the poorer European countries to the richer ones. From 2004 to 2006, around 600,000 went to the UK alone. In 2005, Spain issued 12,000 work permits to Poles, who eagerly snatched up the opportunities for seasonal work with tourists. In 2006, Alicja moved to Barcelona, where her knowledge of English was useful in her job as a waitress: "I met quite a lot of Polish people who came to Barcelona to work just for holidays. Not all of them spoke Spanish but that wasn't necessary. There were a lot of Irish pubs and there one can work even without speaking Spanish. All of us also tried to have fun besides working."

Have Your Say

In the era of globalization, companies can set up businesses anywhere in the world, yet many people do not have the right to freedom of movement because of immigration controls.

- Should people be able to move freely wherever there is work?
- Would this create huge population increases in the wealthiest countries?
- Would this make little difference because only a small minority are able to migrate?

▲ Spain is a popular destination for migrant workers. Here, a Moroccan migrant picks tomatoes. Moroccans account for more than 60 percent of the workforce on Spanish farms.

Immigration Controls

In this era of globalization in migration, nations try to control the number and type of migrants they allow in. Immigration controls were first adopted by countries that experienced mass migration in the late 19th and early 20th centuries. The United States introduced the Chinese Exclusion Act in 1882 to restrict migration from China. In 1905, the United Kingdom passed the Aliens Act to stem the tide of Jewish migrants escaping persecution in eastern Europe. Both countries attempted to deter migrants that they saw as "undesirable"—people who were extremely poor or had radically different customs from the majority of the population.

Few countries had permanent immigration controls until the late 20th century, but by 2000, 40 percent had them. There are immigration controls in LEDCs as well as MEDCs. For instance, to gain permanent residence in Brazil, you need to be either a professional working for a company, running a company yourself, or investing large amounts of money there. You can also immigrate if you are married to a Brazilian or have Brazilian children.

Tough Rules

MEDCs have very strict immigration rules to control the number and the type of people they allow in. Countries such as the UK,

▼ These European immigrants have just passed through the immigration entry station at Ellis Island in New York. Between 1892 and 1924, millions of newcomers to the U.S. came through Ellis Island. In 1924, the Immigration Act restricted the number of immigrants and ended the period of mass immigration.

France, and Germany try to encourage the immigration of highly skilled workers who are needed in their economies, but make it difficult for the less skilled to enter. In France, 64 percent of immigrants are family members who have joined their relatives, while only 12 percent came to do a particular job. In 2006, a law was introduced to restrict family immigration and encourage highly skilled migrants.

After gaining entry to an MEDC, it takes several years to gain citizenship. Some countries, such as the United States and some states of Germany, have introduced citizenship tests. Immigrants are examined on their knowledge of the language and customs of their adopted land before they can become

Eyewitness

"My main reasons for opposing immigration controls are that they are causing great and increasing suffering for many thousands of human beings. Many die in their attempt to reach Europe, in boats, in containers, on the backs of lorries [trucks] or even underneath lorries and planes."
Teresa Hayter, author of *Open Borders* (2004), explains that immigration controls force people to migrate illegally

full citizens. The governments of these MEDCs believe that immigrants who understand the way of life in their host country will fit in better.

▼ These new immigrants are attending a citizenship ceremony in Florida. To become U.S. citizens, immigrants need to live in the U.S. for at least five years, speak good English, understand U.S. history and government, and be of good character.

▲ Yemeni coast guards check a boat full of refugees from Somalia who have fled civil war in their country and made the risky voyage across the Gulf of Aden to the port city of Aden in Yemen.

Illegal Immigration

It is so difficult to meet the requirements for legal immigration to MEDCs that many migrants use an illegal route. Unskilled people know that despite the laws to keep them out, there are many jobs available. They are often in desperate circumstances in their home country, with no chance to make a decent living, so they feel it is worth the enormous risks to migrate illegally. There are an estimated 200,000–400,000 undocumented migrants in France, for example.

Illegal immigration is difficult for governments to control. Where there is a pressing need to migrate, people will somehow find a way. They may pay a people smuggler a vast sum to organize a secret journey, hidden in the back of a van, the hold of a boat, or even the undercarriage of a plane.

Mercy was 20 when she escaped from war-torn Liberia in western Africa with her brother and sister. Traveling on a rickety boat toward Italy with 150 other refugees, one night they were hit by a freak storm and shipwrecked. Many of them, terrified and unable to swim, drowned quickly in the dark waters. A fortunate few, including Mercy and her brother, were rescued and found a home and a welcome in Sicily. Thousands of refugees in leaky boats are drowned each year, their bodies washed up on Europe's beaches. If refugees do arrive safely and their claim to asylum is accepted, they can legally stay in the country. Most remain as illegal immigrants.

Estimates of the Numbers of Migrants (in thousands) for Selected Countries in Five-Year Periods, 1950 to 2000

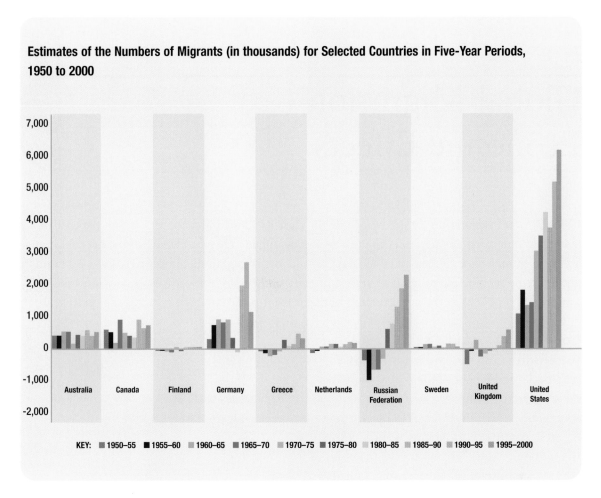

KEY: ■ 1950–55 ■ 1955–60 ■ 1960–65 ■ 1965–70 ■ 1970–75 ■ 1975–80 ■ 1980–85 ■ 1985–90 ■ 1990–95 ■ 1995–2000

▲ This chart gives estimates of the net numbers of migrants—that is, the number of people who entered the country minus the number who left the country. Minus figures mean that more people left the country than entered it.

Tricked and Trafficked

As well as people smugglers, traffickers are criminals who ply their trade among migrants desperate for a better life, often forcing them into illegal work. For example, traffickers deceive young women from Myanmar, China, Laos, and Cambodia with the promise of a good job, but then take them to Thailand to become sex workers or domestic servants. The women are often forced to work like slaves to pay back the trafficker the cost of the trip and to send money to their families back home.

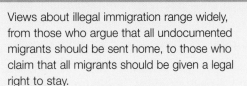

Have Your Say

Views about illegal immigration range widely, from those who argue that all undocumented migrants should be sent home, to those who claim that all migrants should be given a legal right to stay.

- Should governments focus their efforts on stopping illegal immigration?
- If all migration were legal, would this stop people smuggling and trafficking?
- If all migration were legal, would MEDCs be overrun with migrants?

Global Migration – Economic Effects

Globalization in migration can allow people the choice to move to a country where the cost of living and quality of life are better than in their native land. They contribute to the host economy and send money back to their families, too. Yet the loss of highly skilled people causes a "brain drain" in the sending countries. The arrival of large numbers of refugees, especially in LEDCs, can present problems in the host country, both for local people and the refugees themselves.

Good or Bad for LEDCs?

Workers from LEDCs working in MEDCs send back remittances—money that improves the standard of living of their families and communities. Some regions of the world rely on these remittances. Filipinos working in the U.S. not only send back money for their families, but also send contributions to help pay for new parks and libraries in their home towns. The investment of money from abroad in local communities is one of the effects of globalization in migration.

International migration can also help people who cannot find a job in their own country. For instance, there are not enough positions for graduates in India, so the possibility of emigration is useful. India has a huge population of more than one billion, so the loss of emigrants does not have a serious economic effect. The same is true of China. Although about 33 million Chinese live outside their country, this represents only 2.5 percent of the population.

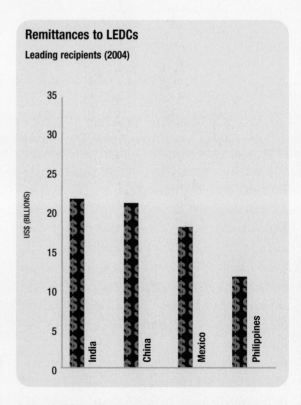

Remittances to LEDCs

Leading recipients (2004)

▲ The bar chart above shows the countries that receive the most remittances, while the chart on page 29 shows the share of remittances received by various regions of the world.

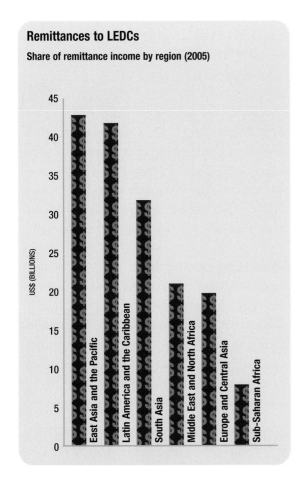

Remittances to LEDCs

Share of remittance income by region (2005)

US$ (BILLIONS)

- East Asia and the Pacific
- Latin America and the Caribbean
- South Asia
- Middle East and North Africa
- Europe and Central Asia
- Sub-Saharan Africa

▲ This teacher of an English class in the UK was recruited from Jamaica. Since World War II, most emigrants from Jamaica have moved to the United Kingdom, although now greater numbers are moving to the United States and Canada.

The Brain Drain

However, emigration can cause problems for small LEDCs, such as the Caribbean islands. Relatively few people in LEDCs receive a good education compared to those in MEDCs, yet highly educated people are the most likely to migrate. About one-third of high school and college graduates from the Caribbean have emigrated, mostly to the U.S. This loss of skilled people is known as the "brain drain." So many nurses and teachers have left that the Caribbean health and education systems are severely short of staff. This lowers the quality of life on the islands and makes it more difficult to achieve economic development. Ultimately, it increases the division between MEDCs and LEDCs.

Eyewitness

"I believe that Jamaica really doesn't foster the talent that we have. The opportunities that are here are limited and so this contributes to the brain drain in our society, where the brightest minds and people who are more innovative, more creative, are leaving. The Americans recognize our talents and they are willing to invest in us."
High-school student Toni-Ann Falconer, *Jamaica Gleaner*, April 6, 2006

Helping their Hosts

Although migration has a mixed effect on LEDCs, migrant workers prove useful to their host countries. They fill gaps in the labor force, at all levels. At the bottom end, they take on the jobs native workers do not want to do. These jobs are sometimes called the "4Ds" because they are "dirty, difficult, demeaning (making people feel small), and dangerous." Many migrants work through the night as office cleaners, in hot fields as fruit pickers, or on dusty, dangerous sites as construction workers. Japan's growing construction and services industries could not run without foreign labor. Construction sites all over the world are full of international migrants. In MEDCs, such as Australia, Canada, the United States, the United Kingdom, and Germany, immigrant professionals are recruited to take on skilled jobs where there are shortages, such as in the health, education, and Information Technology sectors.

Immigrants can benefit the economy in many ways. In general, they pay more in taxes than they take in welfare benefits. They tend to be young and fit, and are usually better educated than the average in the host population. Some are creative and have money to invest in new businesses, which provide employment.

Depending on Migrants

In many MEDCs, important areas of the economy depend on migrant workers. In the U.S. and Spain, the crops would rot in the fields without them. Hospitals and nursing homes across the United Kingdom depend on foreign labor, as do the hotel and catering industries. Scandinavian countries rely on

▲ These South American housekeepers work at the Beverley Hilton Hotel in California, one of the most luxurious hotels in the U.S. Most MEDCs rely on immigrants to do cleaning jobs.

▲ MEDCs increasingly look to immigrants to take on skilled jobs such as working as chefs. The home country has paid for their education and training, but once they emigrate, their skills benefit MEDCs.

migrant health care workers to make up for the shortage of local people prepared to do low-paid nursing jobs.

Like most MEDCs, Australia requires more and more migrants to make up for the decline in growth of the Australian-born population. Stephen Sim came to Melbourne from Singapore as part of Australia's skilled migrant program. His manager had found it hard to recruit a good chef. He was delighted to find Stephen, who was enthusiastic, flexible, and willing to learn.

Focus on...
Immigrants and the Economy

Figures from various countries indicate that over the long term, both legal immigrants and undocumented migrants contribute to the host economy. In Australia, more than 100,000 immigrants and more than 150,000 temporary migrants enter the country each year. Research shows that they contribute more in taxes than they consume in benefits, goods, and services. Undocumented migrants do not receive any benefits because they want to stay hidden from the authorities. Yet taxes are still deducted from their wages, so they are helping to pay for health and education for everyone else.

Stealing Jobs?

There may be some downsides in MEDCs too. Migrants are often prepared to work for lower wages than the native population because the pay is still higher than in their own country.

In the U.S., migration experts such as Peter Capelli from Cornell University, New York, argue that undocumented migrants in particular take jobs away from local people because companies would rather employ them than native workers on higher pay levels. They claim this makes it difficult for the least-skilled American workers to find a job. It may mean that employers fail to invest in new equipment or health and safety measures, and make their employees work in dangerous conditions. Being undocumented, the workers have no one to complain to.

Other experts disagree. A study in 2006 by the Pew Hispanic Center in Waashington, D.C., showed that the increase in migrants did not mean that native-born workers lost their jobs. International migration writer Peter Stalker claims that migrant workers complement native workers. While migrants take on jobs as cleaners, farm hands, and construction workers, local workers move on to more rewarding jobs. Also, the number of jobs in a country is not fixed. Migrants create jobs too. They buy food, ride buses, and spend money on local services, which boosts the economy.

Caring for Refugees

Looking after migrants who arrive as asylum seekers is an expense for the host countries. Although they are often highly qualified, asylum seekers are not allowed to work legally until their claim has been processed. In MEDCs, relatively small numbers of migrants arrive, so the costs of supporting them do not have a huge effect on overall government spending. Over the long term, people who settle as refugees will contribute to the economy of their adopted country.

Focus on...
Economic Effects

Refugees create a demand for services that can improve the local economy, if international agencies help out. In the early 2000s, refugees from the western African civil wars in Liberia, the Ivory Coast, and Sierra Leone flowed to the refugee camp of Kuankan, in relatively safe Guinea. International aid agencies soon followed; the center for their work in eastern Guinea was in Guékédou, a town a few hours' drive away. They spent money locally on food, medicine, translators, and drivers. By 2003, the camp had closed down because of fighting in the area, and the economy of Guékédou had declined dramatically.

▲ Refugees from Sierra Leone in a camp in the Guinea border area, 2001.

However, large numbers of refugees arriving in LEDCs can indeed strain resources. Between early 2006 and early 2007, the ongoing civil war in Iraq displaced 500,000 people from their homes, adding to at least 1.5 million who had already escaped the conflict there. Most are in neighboring Jordan and Syria. Jordan, with a population of 5.6 million and serious economic problems, struggled to cope with at least 700,000 refugees.

Region	Numbers of people
Asia	8,603,600
Africa	5,169,300
Europe	3,666,700
Latin America & Caribbean	2,513,000
North America	716,800
Oceania	82,500
Total	20,751,900

▲ This chart gives the numbers of people that the United Nations High Commission for Refugees (UNHCR) was concerned about in 2006, including refugees, displaced people, and asylum seekers.

▲ An Iraqi refugee in front of his tent in Al-Ruwayshid refugee camp in Jordan, about 46 miles (75 km) from the border with Iraq. During 2007, the conflict continued to worsen, and the number of Iraqis leaving as refugees increased.

Multicultural Societies

When large numbers of migrants come from other countries, there is a significant impact on the community at large. The benefits are a greater understanding and, in many cases, tolerance of people with different cultures and religions, along with a sharing of tastes in food, music, and dance. The drawbacks may be suspicion and resentment of the newcomers, which can lead to racism. Another concern is that in the era of globalization, countries could be losing their national identity.

Resentment

Some people believe that migrants not only steal jobs from local people, but also take up precious health and housing resources, and enjoy welfare benefits at local people's expense.

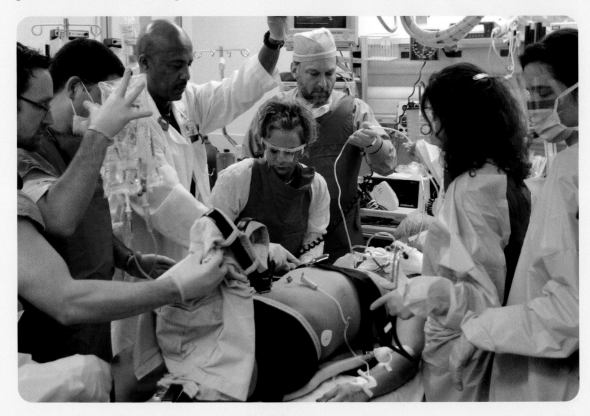

▲ Here, a group of doctors and nurses treat a patient in an emergency room in San Francisco.

▲ Burned-out vehicles litter the streets of the Paris suburb Clichy-sous-Bois after rioting in 2005 over the rights of immigrants.

Research indicates this is generally not the case. A study in 2005 showed that immigrants made up 10.4 percent of the U.S. population, yet only 8 percent of government health care funds were spent on them. In the UK, a Bank of England report in 2007 showed that, "There is little or no evidence to suggest that that the new A8 migrants [from the eastern European countries that joined the EU in 2004] have come to the UK to claim or receive benefits; they have come to work." Nevertheless, the perception of unfairness breeds resentment of migrants. The bitterness has been extended toward refugees as well as migrant workers.

Racism

Immigrants may also feel resentful. In France, for instance, French-born children of families from North Africa believe they are treated as second-class citizens, with fewer rights than native-born people. They suffer racism because of their Muslim background and dark skin, and find it hard to get a decent job. In areas of Clichy-sous-Bois, a suburb of

Eyewitness

"The sons and daughters of Arab and African immigrants face terrible discrimination. Often their CVs [resumes] would be set aside simply because of their names. This racism has bred despair and these youngsters find it difficult to find a route out of poverty."
Antoine, a teacher in the run-down area of Seine-Saint-Denis, France

"The reigning order is too often the order of gangs, drugs, traffickers. The neighborhoods are waiting for firmness but also justice."
French president Nicolas Sarkozy, blaming the immigrants themselves for disorder in their communities

▲ French president Nicolas Sarkozy believes that immigrants are a cause of problems in society. After the riots of 2005, he brought in tough measures to try to reduce illegal immigration.

Paris, half the people are unemployed. In the fall of 2005, the tensions between the immigrant community and the authorities led to the outbreak of serious riots. Over three weeks, damage costing about $350 million was caused to buildings, 10,000 vehicles were destroyed, and nearly 5,000 people were arrested. Such conflict is damaging for society as a whole.

Loss of National Identity?

The racism experienced by immigrants in France is not unique. In many MEDCs with migrant and refugee populations, there are people who want to put a stop to migration. They believe their country is being "swamped" by different cultures and that they are losing their national identity. Since 2001, this concern has often been directed against Muslim migrants. It is one of the effects of the "war on terror," which is trying to stamp out radical Islam and the ideas behind the violent attacks on the U.S. on September 11, 2001.

But some people think that Muslim migrants in general are a problem, whatever their viewpoints. They say Muslim migrants do not fit into society because they keep themselves separate, with their own places of worship, shops, community activities, and ways of dressing. Others argue that Muslims vary in their outlook and habits, just like other people. Many are not even religious. They say that labeling a group of people as "different" in this way is a form of racism, known as Islamophobia, a fear of Islam.

Rise of the Far Right

In many European countries, far-right political parties have taken up the issue of immigration, especially the immigration of Muslims. They encourage Islamophobia to try to win support.

▲ There has been a rise in far-right groups in Russia, which call for "Russia for the Russians." They oppose immigrants and asylum seekers, and carry out violent attacks on them. Here, anti-fascist protesters march to show their opposition to the far right.

▲ Two Palestinian-American colleagues chat on the street in New York City. Their organization provides advice for Arab-Americans, who have come under suspicion since the terrorist attacks of September 11, 2001.

In the Netherlands, for example, five percent of the population are Muslims. A tiny minority of Muslim women wear full top-to-toe Islamic dress. The Party for Freedom, led by Geert Wilders, campaigns for a halt to all immigration and a ban on the building of religious schools and mosques. It wants to outlaw the wearing of Islamic dress by Muslim women. Such campaigns can lead to further divisions between Muslims and the wider society. A poll in the Netherlands in 2006 showed that 63 percent of Dutch people thought that Islam did not fit with modern European life.

Have Your Say

Some people think that globalization in migration means countries lose their national identity, while others believe there is no such thing as a single national identity.

- Are there certain characteristics that make each country different from others?
- Do people share a national identity, or do they have different identities depending on factors such as the region in which they live and their social class?
- Does migration mean that people in the host country will lose their culture?

▲ A woman injured during the bombing of Sarajevo in 1992 is carried into a car to take her to the hospital. The city was under siege from May 1992 until February 1996 and was bombed daily. It is estimated that more than 10,000 people died, and more than 50,000 were wounded.

Difficulties Migrants Face

Whether or not migrants receive a friendly or a hostile welcome, migration is a stressful experience, especially for refugees. Many are suffering trauma and perhaps physical injuries from the violence and persecution they have endured in their own country. They often have to learn a new language and adapt to strange food and a different climate. Zlata Filopovic had to flee Bosnia during the civil war. She was 13. When war hit her city of Sarajevo in 1992, there were gunmen fighting in the streets and it was too dangerous for her to leave the house. At home, the power had been cut off, and it was dark and cold. With the help of friends in Western Europe, Zlata and her family managed to reach Dublin, Ireland. There she was safe and could go to school, although it was not easy to adapt. Life was much harder than it had been when she was growing up. Also, she had to cope with the memories of the death and destruction she had witnessed.

Bottom of the Heap

Once settled, new migrants usually find themselves at the bottom of society, especially until they know the language fluently. They tend to live in the poorest areas in run-down housing. They receive low pay rates and often work long hours in poor conditions.

Migrants generally earn more money than they did in their home countries, but even if they are professionals, they may be forced to take menial jobs. Perhaps their qualifications are not recognized in the new country, or it is hard to find a good job because of racism among potential employers. A 2005 survey in London showed that half of the migrants working in low-paid cleaning, catering, or food-processing jobs had college degrees.

Over generations, however, migrant communities have proved that they generally adapt well to their new country and their situation gradually improves as they become accustomed to the cultural differences. Their children grow up and are educated in the host country; they have better job opportunities than their parents.

Eyewitness

"Suddenly having a life that is often more difficult than the one you grew up with is really hard. Becoming a refugee or simply running away from war is a little war of its own . . . Having to face that scale of death at an early age is a huge trauma for young people. I will always remember so many things because it has totally defined my life."
Zlata Filopovic, Save the Children UK

▼ This cleaner works at night cleaning a subway station on the London Underground. Over half of the cleaners on the Underground are black African immigrants, while 15 percent are from eastern Europe.

▲ At this school in England, more than three-quarters of the children speak English as a second language—between them they speak more than 40 languages. When children from different backgrounds attend school together, they can learn about different cultures and develop respect for each other.

A Richer Society

Over time, migration can enrich society economically and culturally. In the United States, around 15 percent of the population is Hispanic—they or their families are from Latin America. A report in 2006 indicated that the number of Hispanic-owned businesses was growing three times faster than the national average, providing jobs and boosting the economy.

Immigrants have introduced variety into all areas of culture. In Canada in the 19th and 20th centuries, for example, French, English, and Irish settlers all brought their own folk music, while African-Americans developed jazz and blues. More recent immigrants from the Balkans and Turkey have introduced their own musical styles. In 2005, two-thirds of immigrants to Canada were Asian. Nowadays, native-born Canadians are more adventurous in their eating habits. Vancouver has excellent Chinese and Indian restaurants, thanks to the large immigrant populations.

Migration Is Here to Stay

It is clear that international migration has both positive and negative effects. Yet whether or not people think it is a good or a bad thing, it is sure to continue as long as war and persecution occur, and there are wealth gaps between and within countries.

Worldwide, there are many problems to solve. With the improved communications between countries that globalization brings, all nations could work together to reduce conflict and poverty. Then fewer people would be forced to migrate, and people would migrate through choice rather than necessity. It depends on whether governments are prepared to do this, which in turn depends on people making their voices heard.

Doing Your Part

People of any age can become involved in this issue in their local community, through their school, college, workplace, or family. They can gather information about migration and hold a debate on the subject, or take part in volunteer work, sports, or social activities with local migrants. Many organizations, such as Oxfam and the Fair Trade Movement, help poor people around the world to improve their lives. There are many ways to make a difference.

Focus on...
Famous Immigrants

In various walks of life, immigrants have made an enormous contribution to their host country. In the U.S., many famous athletes, writers, actors, business people, and politicians arrived as immigrants. Lenny Krayzelburg, a swimmer from Russia, has won the Olympic gold medal for backstroke three times. Edwidge Danticat left Haiti when she was 12 and later became a novelist. Midori, from Japan, is one of the world's leading violinists; she performs more than 100 concerts worldwide every year.

▲ Lenny Krayzelburg, a Russian swimmer who came to the U.S., is competing in New York. In the 2004 Summer Olympics, there were 25 immigrants and a similar number of children of immigrants on the U.S. team. Several of the coaches were immigrants too.

The Great Debate

Globalization has made it easier for people to migrate, whether they choose to do so because there are better employment opportunities elsewhere, or because they are escaping from war, poverty, or persecution in their native countries. There are both advantages and disadvantages to international migration.

Advantages include:

● People can move to other places to escape poverty, persecution, or war, or simply to find a better lifestyle.

● If there are not enough jobs in their home country, people can move to places where workers are needed.

● Migrants contribute to the host economy, filling the gaps in the workforce.

● Migrants help their families back home with remittances.

● Migration can enable people to join family and friends living abroad.

● When different peoples mix, they find out about each other's customs, enjoy new forms of cultural exchange, and can learn tolerance toward one another.

Disadvantages include:

● Many people are pushed to migrate because economic changes, such as falling prices for agricultural goods, force them to give up their land.

● It is hard to leave behind a home and relatives and move to another country, perhaps never to return.

● There are huge restrictions on who can move legally; many move illegally and at great personal risk.

● The brain drain from LEDCs deprives them of skilled workers.

● Migrant workers are often not welcomed and suffer discrimination.

● Large numbers of refugees place a burden on the countries in which they settle.

Facts and Figures

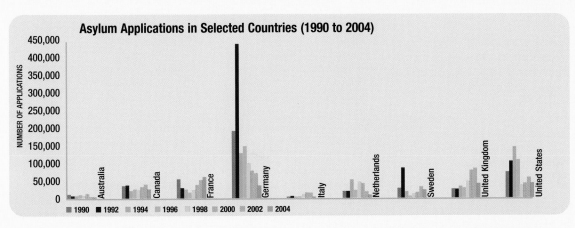

Asylum Applications in Selected Countries (1990 to 2004)

NUMBER OF APPLICATIONS

1990 1992 1994 1996 1998 2000 2002 2004

▲ This chart shows the number of asylum seekers in different countries. The large number in 1992 was because of the outbreak of war in Bosnia.

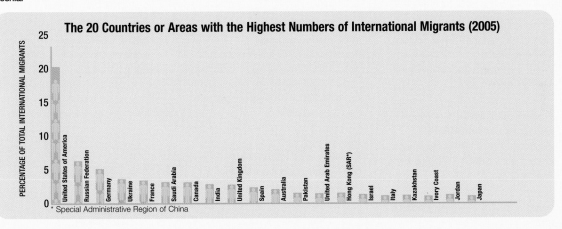

The 20 Countries or Areas with the Highest Numbers of International Migrants (2005)

PERCENTAGE OF TOTAL INTERNATIONAL MIGRANTS

* Special Administrative Region of China

- Number of migrants worldwide in 2005: **191 million**
- Percentage of the world population: **3 percent**
- Percentage of women migrants: **49.6 percent**
- Estimated number of undocumented migrants worldwide: **30–40 million (2003)**
- Estimated number of undocumented migrants in Europe: **7–8 million**
- Estimated number of undocumented migrants in the U.S.: **10.3 million**
- Number of IDPs: **23.7 million in 50 countries**
- Number of refugees: **8.4 million cared for by the United Nations High Commissioner for Refugees and 4.3 million Palestinians cared for by the United Nations Relief and Works Agency**

Further Information

Books

Braun, Eric. *Colombians in America.* In America. Minneapolis: Lerner, 2007.

Egendorf, Laura K., ed. *Illegal Immigration: An Opposing Viewpoints Guide.* Farmington Hills, Mich.: Greenhaven Press/Thomson Gale, 2007.

Hernandez, Roger E. *Immigration.* Gallup Major Trends and Events. Philadelphia: Mason Crest Publishers, 2007.

Libal, Autumn. *Cuban Americans: Exiles from an Island Home.* Hispanic Heritage. Philadelphia: Mason Crest Publishers, 2006.

Libal, Joyce. *Migrant Youth: Falling Between the Cracks.* Youth in Rural North America. Philadelphia: Mason Crest Publishers, 2007.

Ouellette, Jeannine. *A Day without Immigrants: Rallying Behind America's Newcomers.* Snapshots in History. Minneapolis: Compass Point Books, 2008.

Senker, Cath. *Immigration.* Ethical Debates. New York: Rosen, 2007.

Teichmann, Iris. *Immigration and Asylum.* In the News. North Mankato, Minn: Smart Apple Media, 2003.

Web Sites

www.uscis.gov
U.S. Citizenship and Immigration Services—the U.S. government agency that deals with most immigration, refugee, and asylum issues

www.fairtradefederation.org
A U.S. association of fair trade wholesalers, retailers, and producers that aims to provide fair wages and employment opportunities to people worldwide.

www.state.gov/g/prm/
U.S. Department of State, Bureau of Population, Refugees, and Migration is a U.S. agency that formulates policies on population, refugees, and migration and administers U.S. refugee assistance and admissions programs.

http://pewhispanic.org/
A non-partisan research organization which tries to improve understanding of the U.S. Hispanic population and to chronicle Latinos' growing impact on the entire nation.

www.cis.org/
An independent, non-partisan, non-profit research organization that conducts research and policy analysis of the economic, social, demographic, fiscal, and other impacts of immigration on the United States.

www.migrationinformation.org
Migration Information Source: Information supplied by the Migration Policy Institute, an independent think-tank that studies the movement of people worldwide.

Teaching Resources

www.choices.edu/resources/twtn_immigration.php
A lesson plan designed to teach students about current debates in immigration policy.

http://pclt.cis.yale.edu/ynhti/curriculum/units/1996/4/
Remaking America: Contemporary U.S. Immigration offers eleven curriculum units on recent immigration topics, from the Yale-New Haven Teachers Institute.

www.pbs.org/independentlens/newamericans/foreducators.html
The educators' section of this PBS site offers lessons plans for the online educational adventure The New Americans.

www.teachingforchange.org/in_the_classroom/teaching_about_inmigration.html
This site lists Internet links, books, and videos that teachers can use in the classroom to teach about immigration.

Glossary

aid agency an organization that helps a country or area in need, for example, providing food, medicine and shelter.

alien foreign, or someone from a foreign country.

asylum protection for people who had to flee their country because they were in danger.

asylum seeker a person who has escaped his or her country and claims asylum—the right to protection as a refugee—in a safe country.

brain drain the movement of highly skilled and qualified people to a country where they can earn more money and live in better conditions.

citizenship the legal right to belong to a country, either as a person born there or as an immigrant who has gained the right to citizenship.

civil war a war between groups of people within the same country.

colony a land ruled by another country.

deportation the sending back of people to their own countries because they have no legal right to stay.

detention center a secure place, like a prison. Many governments keep asylum seekers in detention centers to stop them from disappearing before their claim has been dealt with.

discrimination treating people unfairly, for example because of their skin color, religion, gender, or age.

displaced forced to leave home and move to another part of the country

emigrant a person who has moved permanently to another country.

ethnic minority group a group that has a different national or racial origin or culture from the majority in a country.

European Union (EU) the political and economic union of European states. In 2007, there were 27 member countries. People within the EU are allowed to live, travel, and work in the different member countries.

globalization the freedom of businesses to operate all over the world and to invest and employ workers wherever they choose.

host country a country that receives migrants and refugees.

human rights the basic rights that everyone should have to be treated fairly, especially by their government.

immigrant a person who has settled permanently in another country, either a legal immigrant who has permission to settle or an undocumented migrant who has won the right to stay legally.

Internally Displaced Person (IDP) a person who had to leave the area where he or she lived and move to a different part of the country.

Islamophobia racism against Muslims because of their religion.

less economically developed country (LEDC) one of the poorer countries of the world. LEDCs include all of Africa, Asia (except for Japan), Latin America and the Caribbean, and Melanesia, Micronesia, and Polynesia.

malnourished in poor health because of lack of food or lack of healthy food.

migrant a person who moves to another country for a limited time.

militia a military force that is raised from the civilian population to help the regular army.

more economically developed country (MEDC) one of the richer countries of the world. MEDCs include all of Europe, North America, Australia, New Zealand and Japan.

people smuggler a person who smuggles migrants into another country in return for a high fee.

permit an official document, for example, one that allows a person to live or work in a country.

persecution the cruel treatment of people, for example, because of their skin color, religion or political beliefs.

racism the unfair treatment of people of a different race.

refugee a person who has been forced to leave a country because of war, natural disaster or bad treatment.

refugee camp a shelter for refugees, usually set up by governments or international aid agencies.

remittances money sent by a relative working abroad to his or her family back home.

residence permission to live in another country.

torture causing a person severe pain to punish him or her, or make the person say or do something.

trafficker generally, a criminal who deceives people into leaving their own country and forces them into illegal work.

transnational company a company that works in several different countries, especially a large and powerful company.

undocumented migrant (illegal immigrant) a person who has not entered the country according to the immigration laws.

visa a stamp in a person's passport made by officials of a foreign country, which allows the person to enter or leave that country.

welfare benefits money provided by the government to people who need help, for example, because they are unemployed, ill, or have young children.

Index